St. Helens Libraries

Please return / renew this item by the las
Books may also be renewed by phone ar
Telephone – (01744) 676954 or 677822
Email – centrallibrary@sthelens.gov.uk
Online – http://eps.sthelens.gov.uk/rooms

1 9 JUN 2014

10 July 2014

1 AUG 2014

1 4 OCT 2014

– 2 DEC 2016

St.Helens Council

St Helens Local History & Archives Library

available for loan

ST.HELENS COMMUNITY LIBRARY

3 8055 01277 7272

The author would like to acknowledge Liverpool Record Office, Liverpool Libraries, for providing the map featured on the front cover and page 8, the National Union of Mineworkers Yorkshire Area for providing the photograph of the pit headgear featured on the front cover, and Andrew Wallace for his historical knowledge of transport in the Liverpool region.

The author would also like to express his heartfelt thanks to Joy Grainge of Wirral Business Services and Wendy Cain for their diligent services.

First Published 2011 by Countyvise Ltd
14 Appin Road, Birkenhead, CH41 9HH

Copyright © 2011 John Connor

The right of John Connor to be identified as the author of this work has been asserted by him in accordance with the Copyright, Design and Patents Act 1988.

British Library Cataloguing in Publication Data.
A catalogue record for this book is available from the British Library.

ISBN 978 1 906823 52 8

All rights reserved. No part of this publication may be reproduced, stored in a retrieval system, or transmitted, in any other form, or by any other means, electronic, chemical, mechanic, photograph copying, recording or otherwise, without the prior permission of the publisher.

I wish to dedicate this book to Pat Clarke with whom I shared so much joy, love and wisdom. Before she died two doctors refused her a brain scan and she died from a burst aneurysm. She was 53 years of age.

CONTENTS

Foreword	1
CHILDHOOD	5
My Photograph	7
The Cast Iron Shore	9
MANHOOD	17
The Man With the Money	19
SUTTON MANOR COLLIERY	23
Beauty in the Ugly	25
The Reluctant Miner	27
Corbusier's Dream	41
THE JOURNEY	45
The Journey to Aracena	47
Trapped	57

FOREWORD

My early days in Liverpool as an apprentice plumber gave me the opportunity to learn the geography of Liverpool streets, roads and its many beautiful buildings, including elegant parks, landmarks like the Liver Buildings and the fourteen miles of overhead railway which ran the full length of Liverpool docks, taking dockers and ship repair workers to their places of work. I remember the railway being on stilts and on Sundays my brother Tom and I went with my father on the Overhead Railway, enabling us to view the dozens of cargo ships and liners. I often travelled on it as a young plumber, and on one occasion I travelled on it when I was employed on the very beautiful liner, the ss *Mauritania*. Unfortunately the Overhead Railway was later scrapped; we can build nuclear weapons, but we cannot afford to re-build a beautiful and practical railway, which would have attracted thousands of tourists, as well as local passengers.

My early Liverpool memories were a mixture of fear and anxieties, experiencing the bombing of the Second World War. I was seven years old and missing my dad, who was in the army. Despite this, my brother Tom and my Mam were a tight-knit family and looked after each other. In the air raid shelter at night and the following morning I would be collecting shrapnel from the streets, mainly from the shells fired by the army Ack-Ack units protecting us from the enemy bombers – they made us feel safe. Although one night we were very lucky. We were in our neighbour's, the Cavanagh's basement air raid shelter when, just a few yards from us, bombers literally flattened six houses and only left a single burning gas pipe from each house. All the people in the houses were killed and our air raid shelter collapsed around us, but that shelter saved all our lives. There was a lot of talk that six retired Jewish ladies lived in the six houses on the opposite side of the road and they were meant to be the targets of the bombing.

The war was tough and the life during that time and in the 1950s was often very hard, although I only became fully aware of it as I got older and more aware of the improvements. After the war my dad was often unemployed, although he was a building tradesman and it often made life very difficult. My mother's parents and their family of nine only lived two doors away and therefore we were a close extended family unit and very supportive of each other.

The early pleasures of my childhood included travelling in Liverpool by tram, being a Cub and a Sea Scout and spending time at places like the Cast Iron Shore on the banks of the River Mersey. I loved Liverpool 8 where I was born and I loved the people, yes, Catholics and Protestants, despite the tensions from both marches and parades, which often created so many problems. These characteristics of Liverpool I know have helped me to be the person I am now and I suppose I was lucky enough to have been born into a family of both Catholics and Protestants.

Later one of my joys in life was leaving Toxteth Technical Institute to become a plumbing apprentice and starting work with 150 other plumbers and apprentices. Here I joined the Plumbing Trades Union and later became a Delegate to the Liverpool Trades Council and Labour Party. These were very exciting times for me and some years later I became one of the youngest Trade Union Officers in the Labour Movement. I lasted one year. I missed the other plumbers I had worked with and couldn't get along with the other officials, as they seemed to be moving in a different class direction from that of our members.

When I had finished my apprenticeship I was due to do my National Service and chose to do 5 years in the coalmines instead of 2 years in the Armed Forces. I was employed in 2 collieries during the 5 years, Sutton Manor Colliery at St Helens and Cronton Colliery on the boundary of Liverpool. My first colliery, Sutton Manor, involved me in a disaster where fortunately no lives were lost and nobody was hurt. It was here that I did all my basic training, including haulage, road repair, coalface training and, eventually, tunnelling and development. It was at Sutton Manor where I was involved in the Main Haulage disaster, when the steel haulage 'rope' broke twice! I have written about this in my 'Reluctant Miner' short story.

Later I transferred to Cronton Colliery where I was employed as a tunneller. For some time at this colliery I had listened to older miners telling us that the water on the coal faces had been caused by some of the old coal owners flooding their pits so they could not be used 'for coaling' after the 1926 General Strike. The hatred between the coal owners and the miners ran very deep in those days and reminded them of how they were starving and had to scavenge for food. One day our tunnelling team and a group of engineers were instructed to drive a small tunnel to see if we could locate the water that was causing such dreadful working conditions on the coal faces and to see if we might be able to improve those conditions. Were we surprised? We certainly were, because we had never believed the stories told to us by the older men.

So we drove a 20-foot long steel arched tunnel with a 6-foot block of concrete with a 4-inch steel pipe running through the concrete, with a stop-valve screwed to the end of the pipe. The 4-inch pipe was then laid to the surface and the whole set-up was connected to a powerful suction pump. The engineers then began to drill through the stopcock and through the pipe, a procedure that continued for many days until one day somebody shouted 'Eureka' and water was flooding everywhere. We were told by telephone that the pipe going up the Main Brew and then up the shaft to the surface was working fine. We and the management were jubilant and in a few weeks the coalfaces were beginning to dry out and we had defeated the old coal owners!

And so I moved on to job after job, profession to profession, constantly enquiring, trying to identify the most suitable employment for me and every place spurred me on to find more interesting and more satisfying places to be. You might find it interesting to read my poem 'Trapped'.

Continuing my journey to find happiness and satisfaction.

Childhood

Mam was bending over the kitchen fire, already she was preparing the evening meal, an all-day simmering scouse.

JOHN CONNOR

MY PHOTOGRAPH

Little John,
With your gold curly hair,
And your lovely, but miserable face.
Why do you frown,
And not smile,
Are you unhappy?
Is your life not good?
Are your family not
Loving and caring?
You are nice and clean,
And have good clothes,
So what ails you?
"I don't know!"
"I am hoping <u>you</u> will <u>tell</u> <u>me</u>!"

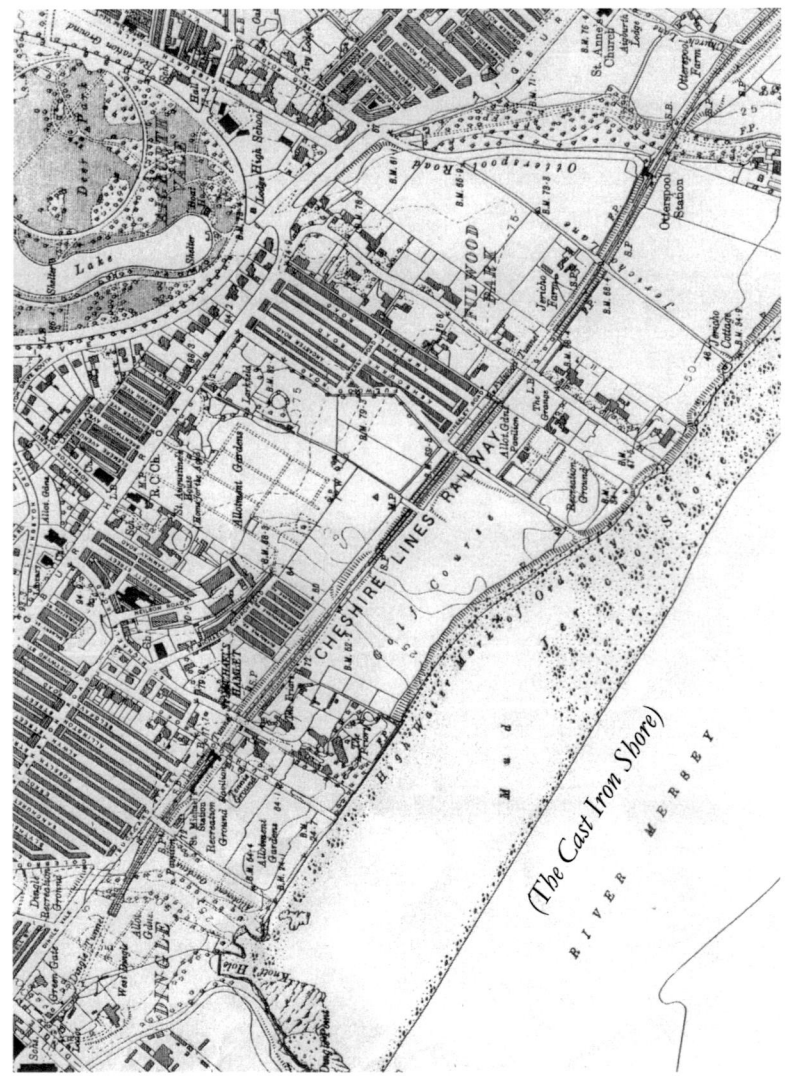

THE CAST IRON SHORE

I woke early, it was Saturday morning "No school today" I said through my big yawn. I had a wash, dressed and went downstairs. Mam was bending over the kitchen fire, already she was preparing the evening meal, an all-day simmering scouse. It was being made from lamb bones, with sliced potatoes, carrots and onions. Oh, lovely, I can't wait!

The kitchen was warm as I sat down at the dining table with my younger brother, Tom. For breakfast we had Kelloggs cornflakes, boiled eggs and finished with toast and jam and a steaming cup of tea. The windows were steamed-up as we didn't have central heating, so I knew it was cold outside. I put on my cap, heavy overcoat and scarf. My overcoat went past my knees, so kept me very warm. My Mam was in the back kitchen, where she did the washing in a copper, heated by a wood fire. She worked very hard doing the washing, cleaning, cooking and shopping for food. Her name was Elizabeth, but everybody called her Lizzie. My Dad was called John and was a painter and decorator. His was also a hard job and affected his breathing. "I'm off Mam" I shouted, "I'm going to the Cast Iron Shore with Jimmy Jones. See you about five". "Bye, John" she replied "have a nice time – don't forget your sandwiches". She had made up a sandwich box with two sandwiches, an apple and a packet of crisps with a bottle of lemonade. "Thanks" I called back, put it into my bag and slung it over my shoulder.

I ran around the corner to Jimmy's house – bbrr, it was cold. I knocked on the door and he came out almost immediately. "Hi" he said. "Hello" I replied, "have you got your lunch?" I asked. "Oh, gosh, no" he gasped. "Mam" he shouted as he ran back along the lobby, returning with his sandwich box down the front of his heavy black jacket. I took it off him and put it in my shoulder bag with my food.

Within five minutes we had reached Park Road where we caught the number 20 tram to Aigburth, from where we would walk to the Cast Iron Shore. Park Road is full of small shops, so riding along it, looking from left to right and right to left, trying not to miss a shop as we drove along was like sitting in the middle of a kaleidoscope of exciting colourful moving pictures. Sturlas Clothes and Shoe shop, and next door Cohen's Olive Oil shop from where my Mam bought olive oil and raspberry vinegar which she gave us every night "to make us big, strong and healthy"! On Sundays, when all the other Christian shops were closed, sometimes she would send me to Cohen's to buy her a pair of nylon stockings. I loved going in this shop because compared with other shops it had an unusual feel and smell; it was like being in a different country or even world. On the opposite side of the road there was a shop where you could buy a single cigarette for one penny! Next door there was a Ladies Hairdressers advertising 'Perms for the Retired'. "What's a perm?" I asked Jimmy. "Dunno" said Jimmy without much interest, quickly adding "I think my sister has one", which ended our conversation about perms.

As we raced along we passed the fruit and vegetable shop with cheap fruit called 'fades', Pegrams grocers and the exciting Home and Colonial grocers. The Home and Colonial had gas lighting, it sold sugar that was weighed and poured into blue paper bags from large sacks, as were biscuits that were displayed in large tins with glass see-through lids. Whenever I went with my Mam shopping to 'the Colonial', the people serving there always gave me small pieces of cheese, boiled ham, corned beef and brawn (pigs head and feet) to eat. They called me 'Little Gimme' – I wonder why? I loved going into that shop! Next door there was a Dewhursts butchers where there were large carcases of different kinds of meat hanging from the ceiling with sawdust scattered over the floor. Then the fish and chip shop where I was sometimes allowed to buy my tea. Oh! We almost missed the Dinky toy shop where they sold Meccano cars and model trains. Too quickly we had passed the shops and were now whizzing past the Gaumont Cinema in the Dingle where I sometimes went on a Saturday morning to the children's performance. It was there I saw 'The Clay Men' (who melted into walls) and it was very, very scary. It was there I also saw 'The Wizard of Oz' and 'Flash Gordon'.

Turning into Aigburth Road, we passed The Toxteth Technical Institute, which later I attended, and was called locally 'Tochy Tech'. It was here where young students of engineering and building technology learnt their trades. Future shipbuilders learned to plan, design, weld, rivet, install lighting on the liners that were built at the local Cammell Laird's shipyard. The building students were taught bricklaying, plastering, woodwork, lighting, plumbing, painting and all it was necessary to know to construct buildings. It was a fine college.

We continued at great speed along Aigburth Road to Lark Lane where we left the tram, thanking the conductor, and followed the road past the Mayfair Cinema, towards the River Mersey. Here we were about six miles from the Liverpool city centre with its many large stores, theatres, cinemas, churches, museums and art galleries, open all day and full of people. We knew we were close to the river because we had started to smell its seaweady salty smell. 'Whoo-whoo' - we suddenly heard a ship's horn blowing off. It sounded like a big ship and then what sounded like a smaller ship replied with 'whoop-whoop-whoop-whoop' indicating she had heeded the warning. "Listen to that" said Jimmy, as we hurried towards the shore. There were large houses either side of the road, almost down to the edge of the river. Sea captains and even shipping line owners lived in these splendid houses.

At last, there it was, the River Mersey about a mile wide and stretching from beyond Warrington and widening as it flowed down to become the Irish Sea. Its salty smell was gorgeous.

Jimmy and I were speechless as we watched the oil tankers waiting to dock at the oil terminal on the Wirral Peninsula on the opposite shore. There were also cargo boats from Sweden carrying timber, and a Blue Funnel cargo ship heading towards Garston Dock, two miles upstream. The cargo ship was being pulled or guided by tug boats, we couldn't tell which. There were also a few small pleasure boats with sails. There was a footpath along the riverbank, with trees behind it. It was an attractive spot, so we found a place to sit and observe the activity on the river.

The tide was high and the river was strong and swelling and from time to time it rose and huge soft waves splashed over us. Whenever this happened we ran into the trees and bushes behind us, returning when it seemed safe to do so; then ran away when it happened again. It was great fun and the only danger if we stayed and sat there was that we would get very wet!

Some time after our arrival two slightly older boys walked along the path towards us, "Hello Lar (Liverpool slang for 'Lad'), worruadoin" said one of the boys in a rich Liverpoool accent. "We're just watching the ships on the river" I replied. "Cum wid us, we're going ter light a fire and make a veg stew". I looked at Jimmy, he didn't seem sure and neither did I, but we both smiled and Jimmy said "Alright, we'll go with you two and you can share our sandwiches". The second boy said "Sarnies ay, that's great".

Their names were Bill and Richard. We walked until we reached a clearing with a large concrete base. It looked like the foundations of an old cottage where fires had been before. The first thing we did was to collect kindling for the fire and then Jimmy and I prepared the vegetables while Bill and Richard built a strong blazing fire.

Bill opened the fairly big rucksack he had been carrying on his back. He took out a kettle, two enamel cups, an old blackened casserole without a lid and a three cornered frame from which he would hang the casserole over the fire. Bill then exclaimed "Dis is proper camping now, don't yer think so". We all agreed that it was and had a good laugh at Bill being so serious, then continued peeling the vegetables with our Boy Scout pocket knives.

The vegetables included potatoes, carrots, sprouts, squashed tomatoes, turnip and some cabbage leaves they had taken from a cabbage field they "just happened to be walking through"! They were all chopped on an old board, put in the casserole to which Richard then added two crumbled Oxo cubes and a large bottle of water the lads had brought with them. They had no lid but fastened a sheet of greaseproof paper they had brought with them around the top of the casserole. They then punctured holes in the paper to let the steam out.

We sat around the fire talking, sharing experiences and finding out about each other. The one thing that we shared was the fact we were all in the Boy Scouts. My friend Jimmy and I were members of a Sea Scout Troop and spent a lot of time in boats and visiting large cargo ships. Some were British and many of them were foreign, it was very exciting. Bill and Richard were members of a Boy Scout Land Troop and went camping a lot. They regularly visited an organised, semi-wild campsite called Tawd Vale near Ormskirk. Jimmy and I had also visited this wonderful campsite so we had a lot to say and share about it. This camp, to us living in the city, seemed like a wilderness yet, as well as having woods, fields and many overgrown wild places to play and hide in, it had its own tuck shop selling food, milk, sweets, drinks, scouting equipment and presents to take home to our families. The camp also had a huge sheltered hollow where large meetings were held and entertainment was also organised. On our last night there we always had a huge bonfire and sang songs and various people would tell stories. It was a wonderful place for young people.

We had so much to share about this camp, but it had to wait because Bill, who had been stirring and attending to the stew, suddenly said "It's ready, and seeing you two are our guests you can eat first". We thanked them for being so thoughtful and opened our sandwich boxes to share with them. But Richard triumphantly held up their two enamel cups and the two bowls saying "we can all have stew together!" which we did, dipping our butties in the gorgeous tasty stew. We ate in silence, for a long time immersed in the fine flavours and our hunger.

Suddenly our eating reverie was disturbed by an extremely loud 'whoop-whoop-whoop' from a ship's siren on the river, followed by a siren reply from what seemed to be a smaller ship acknowledging her warning. We all dropped our food and ran down to the river to discover why the siren had been blown. It was the Blue Funnel cargo ship with its tugs; it wasn't moving and had been there for two hours. We noticed it was getting dusk and Richard said "Garston dock mustn't be ready for thum, it's getting dark so they're warning other ships and boats that they're there and although her lights are all on she isn't moving; it's a safety warning I suppose". We all agreed, returned to our camp, finished our food and doused the fire with water.

Bill produced a torch and we cleaned the cooking utensils with newspaper, collected any rubbish and then moved off along the path towards the road. Bill was leading because he had the torch, we were silent, happy and contented, it had been a wonderful day. We continued until we got to Lark Lane where we had got off the number 20 tram. Here we all separated because Jimmy and I lived in the Dingle and Bill and Richard lived in Garston which is in the opposite direction. We thanked them, said we hoped we would meet again and went on our separate ways, after we shook hands.

Travelling on the tram along Aigburth Road and Park Road our return journey was totally different. It was nearly completely dark, the street and car lights were all on and the lights from the shops were all ablaze, including coloured twinkling lights. Jimmy and I didn't talk, we just sat, listened to the voices around us and took in the spectacle of the shops. "North Hill Street" the conductor shouted. "C'mon" I said to Jimmy "It's our stop" and we got off shouting "thanks" to the conductor. We crossed the main road to Sturlas Clothes and Shoe shop, and walked along North Hill Street where it was darker. Whenever I walked along North Hill Street at night in the dark I noticed I always walked a little faster.

I left Jimmy at his house, said "goodnight", then ran round the corner to my house. I knocked at the door and Mam answered. She was wearing a pinny and I thought "good, tea must be ready". "Did you and Jimmy have a good day?" she asked. "Yes" I answered, "we met two Land Scouts and had a wonderful day – it was brilliant". "Good, your tea is just ready, go and have a wash". "Oh, thanks, Mam, I'm starving" I said as I breathed in the food smells and the warmth of our kitchen fire.

My dad was back from the match and I gave him and my brother a warm 'hello' and then Mam dished up the gorgeous scouse and we had our tea.

Manhood

I clenched my fists, sat down and stared at the worn green linoleum. I felt ashamed.

THE MAN WITH THE MONEY

I was a plumber, unemployed and broke. I had been on the dole before. Come to think of it, it wasn't the first time I had been skint. This was Liverpool and the lot of the casual building worker. But this time it was different. I was in Liverpool and my wife Maureen was in hospital in London. "Fill in this form, we may help you to visit your wife" suggested a sympathetic clerk at the Dole. So I did.

My depression deepened as I entered the waiting room of the Assistance Board where I saw row after row of grey faces that seemed to fuse into the drab green walls. I panicked at the thought that they were 'people' and I was one of them. I wanted to run. I clenched my fists, sat down and stared at the worn green linoleum. I felt ashamed. Ashamed of being there and yet ashamed that I had thought I was different from the people around me. God, how worried I was, perhaps I did not look like them or maybe they were more worried than me. Children cried and my thoughts crowded and blurred the faces. A crackling voice from a loudspeaker called a name which I couldn't understand and an elderly man shuffled towards a door and went through into the 'Inner Sanctum'.

We slowly propelled ourselves along the wooden forms, our bottoms leaving the wood only when we moved up a form, as the interviewing clerk behind the grill shouted questions to decide who was eligible for Assistance. "He's a bastard"

I thought and clenched my fists again as I heard his growl to a young white girl with two babies. "He's coloured is he? And you're not married. Who's the father of the kids then?" What right has he? – but my thoughts stopped, as I looked straight at the face of the man behind the grill. He had half risen from the chair as he was shouting to the girl that she was "not entitled" and I could see his face above the grill. He was fast approaching sixty, with steel grey hair and a face that had been moulded into the most ugly, frightening shape – by hate? Fear of us? Frustration? Overwork? Or was it an overwhelming responsibility? As the girl argued with him and he began raising his voice, the rest of the waiting room became anxious and restless and began to talk loudly and some shouted abuse at the clerk. The man stood up and leaning over the grill shouted to those waiting to "shut up or get outside". I felt angry and sad. What right has he? But I, like the girl, was helpless. I felt sadness for the girl, the clerk and all of us in the room. We seemed trapped. Trapped by other people or by ourselves colluding with the other men. "Who knows?" I mused.

Nudged out of my reverie by the man next to me I heard the clerk shout "next" and stumbled forward. I handed him the form from the Labour Exchange and he began shouting questions for all to hear. Anger welled up inside me, but I answered him quietly and calmly, telling him about my wife in hospital and that I needed the fare to London. He continued asking questions whilst presumably he was writing the answers on a form. Within a few minutes he told me curtly "you're not entitled", then shouted "next". I was furious. I shouted and demanded a "discretionary payment". Whether it was because I shouted or my knowledge of the law which made him more angry I will never know, but he told me to "leave or I will call the police". "Bring the police or the manager," I shouted angrily. This retort immediately calmed him and he told me to sit down and he would arrange for me to speak to the manager.

I sat down amidst subdued praises from the waiting applicants. "That told the bastard"; "It's about time"; "He's been getting away with it for years" and so it went on like a humming top in my ears. But the old man who I now found myself sitting with was not a bit impressed with my apparent success. "You won't see him yer know". "Who?" I asked. "The Manager" he replied. "You're being given the treatment; by the time they call you the Manager will have gone home". If this was true I was to be allowed to cool off and then sent packing.

It was then 3.0 pm and I had been in the 'Outer Sanctum' since 2.10 pm. At 5.15 pm my name was called through the crackly loudspeaker. I entered the 'Inner Sanctum' and was directed into a large room with a huge semi-circular counter divided into at least a dozen interviewing booths. A young woman called my name, I sat down and she began asking me the questions I had already answered. I explained that I had requested to see the Manager. She looked surprised and told me that the Manager had left the office. Christ, the old man was right! After I explained again the reason for my application the clerk, who was very pleasant and sympathetic, suggested we completed another form. This we did and for a second time I was told I was "not entitled" and "no, I could not have a discretionary payment".

The following morning, after discussing my experience with a councillor friend who sat on an Appeals Tribunal

I went back to the Board, but this time entered by the staff entrance. I found the Manager's office, knocked and entered. He had a pleasant face and an engaging manner. I explained my entry, told him about my experience the day before and that my friend (naming him of course) had confirmed that I could be considered for a discretionary grant. He immediately agreed and suggested he should see if my application was filled in correctly. When he returned he placed the train fare to London in my hand, apologised for the way I had been treated and told me he hoped my wife would soon be well again.

Now I know that the Board employs many different types of people. Some dedicated civil servants, others striving to understand and be fair to people, and there are many quite unsuited to handling people with problems; in particular there are those frustrated failures from other Government Departments who transfer to the Department in the hope of finding success.

Now that I have released my suppressed feelings about the Department, I think I might manage to write objectively about it. The theme – ABOLITION!

Sutton Manor Colliery

So as an alternative to two years in the armed forces, facing physical and spiritual death, I chose five years in the coalmines.

BEAUTY IN THE UGLY

Slag heaps,
Waste from collieries
Dark and ugly.
With shape and colours.
Beautiful cones,
Black, blue and grey,
Glinting with reds and greens.
Reminding me of peacocks,
Beautiful and proud.

Coal, never
A thing of beauty,
But practical,
With use and value.
In winter giving
Heat and pleasure,
Adding joy
To our festivities.

Looking deeply,
Into coal,
Those same
Peacock colours,
Black, blue,
Green and red,
Proudly enhancing
Its shapes.

Coal miners
Observed the colours,
Fashioned shapes,
Sculpting heads, faces, figures,
Trains and cars.
Enhancing the natural
Lumps of coal
Into works of art.

Slag heaps
Smoulder,
Dross from coal
Released
From its captivity.
Millions of years,
Waiting to be liberated
Into the light,
Like people,
Sharing its energy.

Coal and labour,
Converted
Into food, clothing,
Shelter and transport.
So too with slag,
Slag heaps.

Now grasslands,
Parklands
And forested hills.
Coal,
Transformed into wealth,
Slag,
Metamorphosed into places of beauty.

THE RELUCTANT MINER

There was a whirring and crashing noise in my ears and I was being beaten on the shoulder with a great chunk of wood. At least that's what it felt and sounded like. The reality was much worse. My alarm clock had slipped off a plate and fallen into an enamel bucket and my wife was gently shaking my shoulder, and saying, "It's half past four, you'll miss it again!" Christ, it was morning! Worse still, it was Tuesday morning. I always found Tuesday mornings difficult. It had something to do with Monday morning being easy after the weekend, and then getting more and more depressed during the day, so that on Tuesday morning, my unconscious and conscious motivations glued me in the bed. I found Friday a snip. Need you ask why? At 4.30am in the morning, with a bus to catch at 5.30am, there is no time or inclination to be introspective. You either get up or you say, "Bugger it!" and go back to sleep.

"Why go at all? You must be mad!" I was often told. The British government was at war in Malaya and I was at war with the government. I just wanted National Service. I didn't want to kill Malayans and, frankly, I had decided that to die at 21 years of age was far too young. So as an alternative to two years in the armed forces, facing physical and spiritual death, I chose five years in the coalmines. But that is only part of the story. When I went 'down pit', I had just completed my apprenticeship to the plumbing trade and wasn't long married. I had responsibilities. I had a wife and two hire purchase Companies to support!

I was born within the sight and sound of the Protestant Orange Order parades, and the Roman Catholic St Patrick's Day processions. My formative years were spiced with violence and bitterness and laced with ships' sirens and the salt of the Mersey: these smells along the dock road and the sight of ocean-going ships were early joys to my eyes and nostrils. My early experiences were filled with the rich folk history of dockers and seafarers. To find myself a miner, working underground, was strange indeed.

I spent two weeks preparing to go underground Bold Colliery in an underground training gallery, and on the surface, attended lectures, watched films demonstrating men and machines at work; we were also instructed in safety measures that, by law, must be applied, but in practice, were often ignored. After two weeks, I started work 'down pit' as a haulage hand, a trainee under the personal supervision of an experienced miner.

On my first day at Sutton Manor Colliery, I was painfully conscious of my newness and the superior position of my workmates. They knew it. My every move was watched and I was ignored. I was new. Gleaming white helmet, brand new electric lamp and rubber belt to carry my battery, boots with shiny steel toe-protectors, snap tin and water bottle, even my old working clothes appeared new compared with the ragged, sweat-stained clothes of the men around me.

This was a strange new world of smells, accents and tensions. The smell of steam, soap and sweat permeated the locker rooms and showers. Conversations were studded with Irish brogues, Lancashire drawls, guttural tones of East European émigrés and the nasal twang of Liverpudlians.

The on-setter rattled the button and we were plunging down like a stone, in a cage on the end of a steel 'rope' ['rope', in pit language, means a stranded steel flexible cable]. The rope passed around the headgear over the top of the shaft, lapping the drum of a powerful engine, and on the other end, a second cage was bringing up men off the night shift. My knees were slightly bent, so that my legs would not break if the cage stopped suddenly, and my pulse pounded in my head like a pneumatic hammer. It was about 900 yards from the surface to the pit-bottom and, by custom, the journey is made in silence. The silence is only broken by the rush of air and the rattle of the guide ropes as the two cages meet and pass, the guide ropes mercifully preventing the cages from colliding. The only other time I remember the silence being broken was when the 'winder' in his engine-house dropped us too fast and the automatic brake operated. Stopped so suddenly, the cage would continue its journey, stretching the rope and producing the same effect as a broken rope. Result? Sweat, curses – relief!

The cage settled like a bird at the floor level of the pit-bottom. A blaze of lights and a crowd of black faces queuing for the cage, like a mirage. This is the downcast, so there is an icy blast of air coming down the shaft to be distributed round the districts, through the second pit and up the second shaft, the return airway. The pit-bottom, because of the velocity of air, was always cold. Winter or summer, the men working there were red-eyed and well 'clobbered-up'.

I left the crowd and was new again. I was obeying my first instruction, standing outside the under-manager's office. I hadn't long to wait before an official came out of the office, distinguished by his spot lamp, with a long beam and an oil lamp that could be re-lit if it went out. "You the new 'un?" he asked, "where yer from?" My answer, "Liverpool" was not to his liking. "Christ, another one, we never get miners these days." And turning on his heel, he said curtly, "Foller me." He was a tall man with a crumpled face, marked with blue scars, heavily built and with a slight stoop. He moved swiftly but cautiously. In his late fifties, he suffered from silicosis. I was soon to know him well as the day shift over-man, who, like most miners, chewed tobacco and spat juice and spittle in liberal amounts. A delight I later learned to enjoy. The over-man is located in the middle of the colliery management, supported by his under-manager – one for each pit- an over-man on every shift for each pit, and a fireman [officially called a Deputy] and at least one shot-firer for each district on every shift.

From the pit bottom to a mine, appropriately called 'The Inferno', ran a one-and-a-half mile long incline, which was the main haulage artery of the pit. Down this steep brew, empty boxes were lowered and drawn back full of coal or 'dirt' [rock or, literally, anything that isn't coal]. The boxes ran on metal rails, lashed to a thick and endless rope with a chain hooked on to the first and last box in the train. They went down empty in sixes and returned loaded in twos.

My first job was 'taking off' at the top of the main brew close to the pit-bottom. The over-man left me under the supervision of a lad, about 20 years old, who laughed and spat tobacco juice every time I made a mistake. As each set of full boxes arrived on the level, it was my job to unlash them from the rope, when their own weight would then take them into the shunts. From then, up to the surface. Easier than it sounds. I had to jump on the chain to slacken it, pull the lashed chain along the running rope, unlash it and, in one movement, flick the chain so that the link at the end of the chain unhooked from the box. If you weren't fast enough either performing the operation or ringing the bell to stop the rope, then the chain was drawn under a pulley, often causing the boxes to smash into it. Ringing the bell was equally disastrous for the nerves, because it brought down the wrath of every official within sight or sound. You tried like hell not to stop the rope because of the snowball effect it could have throughout the pit. Boxes from the main brew were fed on to endless rope systems in the districts, that were filled with coal from conveyer belts linked to belts on each coalface. A lengthy stop or a series of very brief stops anywhere in the system could cause serious delays, which affected production and the piecework earnings of the colliers, who extracted the coal.

After a week as a pretty hopeless taker-off, fingers intact [I was luckier than others] but my nerves were somewhat frayed. I was transferred to a level of three quarters of a mile down the main brew. The level ran off the main brew at an artificial 'flat' called 'The Pulleys'. When you arrived at The Pulleys, you could continue down to The Inferno, go left to the 'California' district, or right to 'Yard Mine'. The Pulleys fed all the districts with empties.

My second job in the level was much less hectic than the one in the main brew. I was under the supervision of a very tall, pale, Liverpool man, who had worked in the level for four years. Bill was an extremely placid man and, although we couldn't talk when we were working because of the noise from the haulage engine, we became friendly, and he was helpful and eager to teach me.

I was becoming a haulage hand. I could now lash-on and take-off. I had learned to repair rails ripped up by wayward boxes, and even the knack of putting a 10cwt box of coal back on the rails with my back.

I had been in the pit four weeks and I was becoming confident. Too confident. This day, among other days, I will never forget. Bill and I were working in the level as usual, when the haulage rope stopped moving in its slow monotonous fashion, occasionally dropping gently between the rails and sending up balls of dust. The steel rope stopped, but the engine was still pulling. The engine winder [operator] had fallen asleep so he was not aware that the rope had been stopped by a 'grind', and that the full power of the engine was engaged in a struggle with whatever had stopped the rope. The rope vibrated violently, beating the floor and the tops of the boxes like a cobra in mortal combat.

Bill sprang into action, swinging on the bell wire, which ran the entire length of the haulage road, which flashed a light and rang a bell so the winder man knew when to stop or start the engine. Bill pulled on the wire and screamed to the engine winder, "Stop, you silly old bastard! Stop the rope." The rope suddenly went limp and didn't even attempt a life-saving twitch. The winder-man came down from his platform, where the noise of the engine made speech impossible and often lulled him to sleep. He had obviously just wakened from a good kip, where he was probably dreaming of a life far removed from the pit, in a 'clean, healthy, factory'. "Nah, what fookin' 'ell's gooin on?" Bill picking up his road hammer and stuffing his pockets with road nails, shouted back disdainfully, "There's a grind, you silly ould bleeder." "Let's go," he said to me.

A 'grind' is a breakdown in the endless rope system. A rail torn up, a fall of rock, a box catching the side of the roadway or jamming against a low roof. A serious grind, say, a set of boxes jamming 'fast' in the roof and the engine keeps drawing the rope, could stretch and snap the rope, often with disastrous consequences. This I was yet to see.

We walked along the long straight tunnel, carved out of 'grey metal', supported by steel arches every yard. Twelve feet high by ten feet wide. From the entrance to a distance of fifty yards, it was whitewashed and illuminated with electric lights. I liked the level; I felt safe and secure working in it. As we left the lights behind and penetrated deeper into the California workings, Bill unclipped his spot lamp from his helmet and directed it along the tunnel. We trudged in silence through the deep dust, which billowed about us like a sandstorm, caking our nostrils and mouths. "Christ!" I murmured. Bill, sensing my fear, silently handed me his 'screw' of tobacco. I had never chewed before, but I rived a piece off with my teeth and handed it back. I chewed without even remembering to spit out the juice.

Abruptly, Bill stopped. "What is it?" I asked anxiously, squirting out a long stream of tobacco juice. "Nowt," he growled, revealing his own anxiety, moving forward slowly and cautiously. Stopping again, he whispered, "Jesus wept, look at that!" Peering forward, I followed Bill's spot lamp flashing on a huge white and black streaked pot-stone that had dropped, crushing the steel arch supports into the floor and pinning the rope securely. It had completely blocked the tunnel. As Bill moved forward again, there was a sound like hail stones falling on a corrugated roof, and before the dust enveloped us, I could see the roof falling in huge chunks, running towards us.

"Run!" shouted Bill, bumping into me as I stumbled my way out of the 'fall'. Run? I ran the whole length of the level as if I had a rocket chasing my arse! As a miner, this was my first clash with nature. And I won – but only just. My new white helmet was scratched, my shirt and trousers torn. Falling rock had cut my arms and fingers, and my knees were scraped and bleeding from stumbling and falling. But I was alive!

The stone that blocked the tunnel was 14ft high and 11ft wide and 6ft deep, and it took one-and-a-half shifts to clear it and repair the damage. I didn't help in the cleaning up operation. I was so scared, I stayed at home for two days.

Some time after the roof 'fall-up', I received the dubious distinction of graduating to The Pulleys. By that time, I was a fully-trained haulage hand. The Pulleys was the nerve centre of the whole pit. From the pit-bottom to The Inferno mine, this steep brew sucked in three miles of rope, one inch in diameter, spliced into a loop to take empty boxes in and draw 'full 'uns' out. Working at The Pulleys was hell. You never stopped. But I was glad about the move for I was working with a group of men and we were able to talk a little, as well as shout and curse. The language used by miners is the most colourful of all my work experiences. Libidinal excesses, which are tension releasing and deeply ingrained in the culture patters of pit life.

I was now a member of a team. We slowed empties by throwing 'scotches' [solid iron rods] into the spokes of the box wheels. We unlashed them. We 'rived' them round the corner into Yard Mine. To send empties into California, we linked three 6ft long chains together, hooked them onto the first box in a train and lashed the other end onto the California's haulage rope. The rope drew them across the roadway into the level and every time ripped up the riving slates on the floor and smashed into the brick pillars supporting the junction above our heads. Empties were also lashed on the main rope again and sent down to The Inferno. The volume of coal sent up to the surface from the three districts was enormous.

I worked in a team of four. Three haulage hands and a 'pusher-on' [the nearest surface equivalent is a charge-hand]. We lashed-on, took-off, scotched, rived, lifted boxes back on rails, when rails or plates were ripped up, we nailed them back; after small grinds, we repaired the road and cleaned up. Whatever we did, the pusher-on was there to show us how to do it better and faster. He would grab a chain from your hand and lash it on the rope. He would then scream and shout "Move the friggers!" as we sent empties into the blackness of the workings and full boxes of coal towards the daylight. He was a National Coal Board dynamo, a bundle of nerve fibres with a heart of coal.

The day shift over-man visited The Pulleys regularly throughout the shift. He constantly rang to ask the score, and discuss with firemen the state of the coal faces. Whenever he was around, the pushers-on went into a frenzy. If there was a stoppage or any kind of difficulty, the over-man added his aggressive authority to the highly-charged atmosphere. The warning about 'Lights' or 'Travellers' from any member of the team indicated that somebody was travelling down the brew from pit-bottom. They were often senior officials in the under manager, manager or area manager class. They added to the tensions and even the over-man had to be informed if he was around. Though God alone knows what we were supposed to do when they arrived; we certainly couldn't work any harder. I suppose the real purpose was to feed the districts with the information so that they could expect the officials.

The work was hard, the tensions high, but, we were a team who commanded respect for our tenacity and expertise. We had status and were also paid a few coppers a shift 'over the odds'. At 'snap time', our only break of 25 minutes, we had time to eat, drink, talk and, sometimes, doze. The other three were from mining families and I was from Liverpool – an outsider without mining tradition. But they were friendly and even the Pusher-on relaxed for snap. The talk was about bowls, greyhounds, racing pigeons, women, rugby football and pit, pit, and pit. No matter what the subject, it always led back to coal. Coal permeated the whole of their lives and pit conversations continued on the surface, in the canteen, in the homes and in the clubs and pubs. Rarely could I take part. I was determined to become a miner so I listened. I heard about the 'Brig Strike of '26', the scabs and their names, the 'old bosses' – and the 'new' – the merits of various coal faces and arguments about new techniques were ever-present. Stories of explosions, rock falls, gas clouds, water breaking in and 'weights coming on' were told over and over again.

The story of a weight coming on in the California mine was told repeatedly. The seam had a good roof and was five feet high. No doubt there were plenty of cracks and bangs on the face and in the vicinity of the face, as the normal weighting came on, as it does when virgin coal is removed and leaves a gap to be closed. On the day of the weight, there was a distant rumbling, a road and the whole length of the face was reduced to two feet six inches. Iron props were forced into the floor, wooden supports splintered and in the roadways, steel arches were transformed to abstract shapes. The miners fled the district and refused to return.

I spent many hours listening to bawdy stories; about escapades with women; pit folk lore; the miners' version of Union history and their opinion of the Union, which never reached the ballot box. I was learning about the pit, about the men, their families and was struggling to become a miner myself: it wasn't easy.

On the day of my second traumatic experiences in the pit, I was lashing on, standing in the middle of the road with the rope moving past me on either side. Suddenly, without warning, the one inch thick metal rope began to move wildly in all directions. It was hitting the girders in the roof and belting the floor with great thumps. Instead of going up the brew, the boxes of coal I had just lashed on, disappeared below the landing down the dangerously steep incline towards the Inferno. The over-man screamed from the Yard Mine level, "Balls of fire and red ink! Fook off! Fook off!" As the rope hit the roof, the taker-off and I shot into the level towards the over-man, just missing being hit by boxes hurtling past. More boxes roared past and crashed into the brick pillars. The crashing and banging of uncontrolled boxes could be heard higher up the brew. Dust, thick everywhere, made it impossible to see. Water from a burst main could be heard pouring down the incline of The Inferno. "What is it?" I thought. "An earthquake? A rock fall? But the rope? Oh, God knows, I don't." It was beyond me. Then the air began to clear and I could see men beginning to move about. I moved with them, aimlessly, but after the numbness in my brain, which the shock of the experience had produced, it brought me relief.

Bells began ringing, telephones buzzed with activity. The pusher-on was speaking into the telephone, and the overman was shouting instructions to everyone, including the pusher-on. "Check the men are alright. Ring The Inferno, Pit-Bottom, Number Two Level, see if Bill's OK, is Charlie alright?" So he went on giving orders, asking questions and, without any doubt, in absolute command. The rope had broken! It had to be spliced as quickly as possible. The road made ready for coaling again. The job of the miner is to produce coal.

When the main brew was inspected it was discovered that a roof fall the size of a double-decker bus had crushed everything below it, mangling and crushing steel arch supports, steel transport boxes and box guide rails, contributing to the whole disaster.

The full length of the one-and-a-half mile long brew had to be cleared and repaired. Men were brought from all the districts to do what, to me, appeared to be an impossible task. Boxes were piled neatly on top of each other in tiers of three and even four, jammed tightly between floor and roof. Other boxes lay on their sides; rails were uprooted;

arches torn from their positions; coal and rock fallen from the roof and spilled from boxes lay strewn everywhere. It took only three shifts and the brew was cleared, repaired and a brand new one-and-a-quarter inch rope installed, ready for 'coaling'.

Three miles of brand new rope that was reputed to be unbreakable. The other rope had been broken by a grind. Two days later, the new rope also broke! The same chaos occurred again. No life was lost on either occasions. Lucky? Bloody lucky!

He was a National Coal Board dynamo,
  a bundle of nerve fibres with a heart of coal.

CORBUSIER'S DREAM

In the industrial north,
Chemical plants
Competed with coal
For supremacy.
Often nudging close
For space and comfort.

Dangerous places,
The engineer instructs,
"Weld this pipe",
No problem,
"Where's the shutdown?"
"There will be no shutdown,
Production must not cease!"
"It will explode"
His ugly, angry face
Gave his answer.
I left the plant.

New job,
New site,
Same ugly conditions.
Repeated chlorine gassing,
Alarms howling,
We file into the gas shelters.
Watch green clouds
Sweeping past,
Like tall ships,
Escaping,
Dispersing.

The 'All Clear',
Wails resignedly,
We return to work.

The chemical industry
With its dangers,
Poisonous smells,
And ugly conditions
Survived.
But coal
Was brutally
Destroyed.

Chemical plants
Have an attraction,
Their complicated web
Of intricate pipework,
All painted silver.

Paint them
In different colours
And shades,
Colour bands,
Indicating content and flow
Would blend
With pastel shades,
Strong blacks, greens and blues,
Creating abstract patterns,
Blending with the construction.

Producing complex,
Subtle pictures,
Of cities,

Floating,
On beautiful lakes.
Corbusier,
Would be very pleased.

The Journey

This was the beginning of the growth of my psychic experiences...

JOURNEY TO ARACENA

One night in a dream I was shown a series of very beautiful, pale blue underground caves and a voice told me "you are a child of Ra, a magician and a healer". Later outside of the dream I discovered that Ra, the Egyptian Sun God, was believed to have lived in an underground city in Ancient Egypt.

This was the beginning of the growth of my psychic experiences that started after I had been introduced to crystal healing by a healer, Kathleen Huddlestone, to whom I am greatly indebted. Some time later that year I was running a crystal workshop and one of the members of the group, my friend Pat (she later became my partner), whilst holding a piece of citrine to her third eye 'saw' horses running through an orange grove in Andalucia in Spain and felt it had something to do with me. Shortly afterwards I meditated whilst holding the same piece of citrine and my spiritual guide, Mary, spoke to me telling me "You must go to Aracena where there is a cave containing a waterfall and it is where I will be with you". She said that the cave wasn't a holy place, she had never appeared there and Aracena was only famous for its cave, not her appearance.

Nothing like this had ever happened to me before and I really did not know what to believe. I wanted to go, yet frankly felt silly even contemplating going. But, before I could decide to say I wouldn't visit Aracena, Pat, who was a very reluctant clairvoyant, had a further vision about a place she said was called Ronda. My immediate reaction was that it was Rhondda in Wales, but she was quite adamant that it was not in Wales but in Spain. I just shivered, now two places, both in Spain. What Pat was shown was 'a large hole in the ground with water at its bottom. There was something like a church building above it with a bell and beyond it some white buildings with red roofs'. I did a check on whether Aracena and Ronda were in existence and yes, they were, they were both in Spain and Aracena did have a cave. It was then I decided I must go on a spiritual journey to both these places, which are about 100 miles apart. When I rang Pat to tell her about my decision to go to Spain she had actually had a further vision of the 'hole in the ground' and the surrounding buildings. There and then she agreed to do a sketch of it (see the copy of the sketch).

So, there I was in Marbella in Spain. It was 5th January and my birthday, the next day, was Christmas Day in Spain. I was staying at a lovely hotel with all its rooms interlaced with beautiful gardens. Looking up I could see majestic mountains clothed in their winter purple, strong and vibrant. I looked down, the sea was green and angry, surrounded by purple flowers and green and grey olive trees. The air was sweet and balmy, wet with soft warm rain. It was magical and I felt I had been there before.

On arriving at the hotel I was given a brochure for coach trips, including one for Ronda, which is only 30 miles away from the hotel. When I looked at the literature for Ronda I was so amazed and so excited – there was a photograph of Pat's sketch just as she had seen it. It was quite unbelievable;

so much so that I felt quite jittery. I wished Pat had been there to share this exciting phenomenon. But I had become friendly with a couple on the flight, so I decided to share this miracle with them. It was a terrible mistake – they moved away from me as though I was a mad man.

That day I visited Ronda, the Ronda in Pat's vision and sketch and actually stood on the bridge shown in her sketch. Yes, there were white buildings with red roofs as I looked through the bridge. I had to keep reminding myself why I was there, although the real reason why I was there had still to be revealed.

Ronda is a prosperous city situated high in the mountains on a plateau, the city divided by a gorge, the old part on one side and the new on the other. There are beautiful old buildings, a bull-ring and churches, although most of the churches were closed when I tried to enter them. Finally I found an open church that had originally been built as a mosque. It had a huge statue of the Black Madonna, which dominated the whole of the church. I was praying and meditating at the foot of the Madonna when Mary my spiritual guide spoke to me: "Nothing unusual is going to happen to you, just walk around Ronda and enjoy yourself. You need to relax, you need to take in the Celtic energies, and you are here to adapt to new energies on a higher plane". Later in the hotel I felt very relaxed indeed. During the evening in the hotel Mary spoke to me again. She said: "I am going to give you my light" and I saw a long bright light shine into my body. It made me feel very, very good indeed - very relaxed and very happy.

I returned to my hotel in Marbella to make preparations for my trip to Aracena. I travelled by coach to Seville,

Above: A photograph of the Ronda bridge which Pat sketched having never seen it (opposite).
Below: John saw doors very similar to this door when he visited Ronda; large, heavy decorative doors are common-place (see page 55).

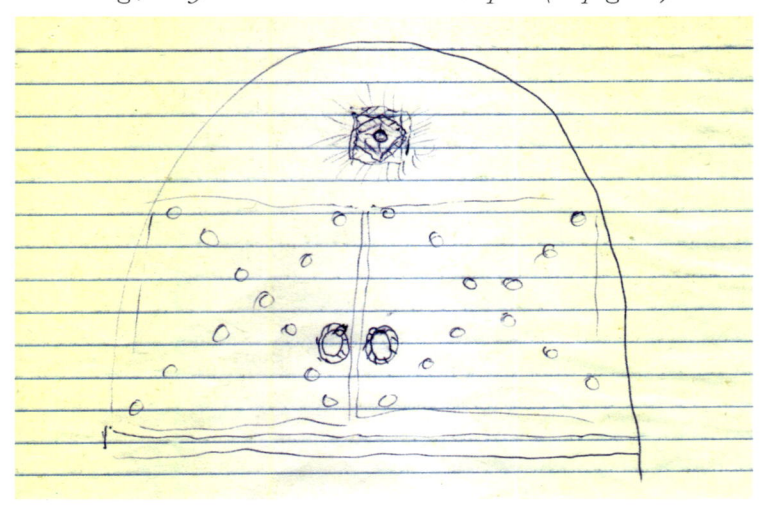

LIVERPOOL MEMORIES

Sketch by Pat from her vision showing one of the Ronda bridges, some of the surrounding area and the gorge.

changed to a local bus and arrived at Aracena in the early evening having travelled just over 200 miles. Aracena is a very pretty place made of stone and very quiet. I booked into a small hotel, later had a very good meal and went to bed early in preparation for the next day at the cave.

The next day I visited the cave or grotto as some local people called it. The director, Señor Santos, conducted me personally. It was strange because as I entered he came walking straight towards me and introduced himself even though there were cave guides waiting. We talked and I eventually decided to tell him why I was visiting the cave. He looked astonished and disbelieving simultaneously and then exploded: "Jesus Christ!" When I asked if he believed me he said: "Why not, all things are possible, even re-incarnation or maybe your family have lived or visited here"! I didn't know for sure, but I didn't think so. He then said he would personally conduct me on the tour of the cave and so I had a personal guide who spoke excellent English.

The cave, or more correctly caves, are unbelievably beautiful, the main grotto having a lake, which is divided, into two parts. Nothing unusual happened until we reached a small cave containing a stalagmite in the shape of a mother holding a child. Mary and the infant Jesus, or Isis and Horus? I just didn't know. What I did know was that it was as though it had been sculpted by an artist, it was stunning and being around it was wonderful. I asked Señor Santos if he minded if I could be on my own for a while and he agreed. I started praying and a voice in my head (I think it was my guide Mary) said "You must learn to be calm and peaceful as it is here. The world needs to be calm and peaceful, but your personal task is to go to the centre of the earth. It is there you will find your answers. You must go to the church above the cave". In seconds I felt calm and peaceful and so wonderful.

The church above the cave was alongside a castle built in the Middle Ages. Señor Santos told me that in the past the Knights Templar lived in the church and in those days it was probably a military base. From the castle and church you can see for miles around Aracena and whilst I was sitting outside the church I suddenly had a vision of a beautiful arched ceiling and a large circular glass window; my inner voice said "This is the multi-arched ceiling of the large hall" and nothing else!

Later when I went into the church I was astonished to see the same ceiling in stone with the circular glass window. The second church I visited in Aracena was totally dominated by Mary the Mother of Jesus, so much so that there were 3 statues of Jesus in the body of the church as well as a picture of Him. In a meditation I asked whether there was a connection between me, the church and the multi-arched ceiling and my inner voice told me "You were a captain in the Knights Templar based at Aracena and you sat at the High Table in the large hall. You were a very brave and strong person then, but you are not now. We have brought you to Aracena to see if you can regain some of that strength". In the hotel later that evening I had a further vision, this time of Mary's Blue Bush, which she first showed me when I was on retreat on the Island of Iona in Scotland. This time she said, "I am showing you the Blue Bush so you know it is me, listen and be calm. Coming to Aracena is to teach you to be calm. I will now give you my light". Then I felt and saw the light as I did at Iona. I also noticed that evening that my hair had a golden sheen to it, which it did not normally have.

After having a meal that evening and relaxing a voice in my head told me that the connection with Pat and Ronda and myself was that: "You met when you were in hospital here and she was a nursing sister. Her name then was Sister Clare Gonzales (in this life she was Patricia Clark and died on 11 March 1998), you fell in love but were never lovers". I felt wonderful.

The following morning when I was sitting on the bus going back to Seville at 7.45 looking at the red sun coming up behind the castle and the church I didn't want to leave this beautiful place. Suddenly my inner voice spoke to me: "You were a captain in the Knights Templar, your name was James Ferdinand. You were wounded in a battle and were nursed by Pat who was a religious nursing sister, Sister Clare Gonzales. She nursed you in hospital at Ronda". I was getting used to the voices, but this information was just mind-blowing. I was reminded that my friend Kathleen, who is a healer and clairvoyant, once told me that she believed I had been a Knight Templar in a previous life. I sat on the bus absolutely stunned with nobody to share it. I wished dearly that Pat had been with me. During my journey back to Marbella I decided to make a further journey to Ronda because it now seemed possible that, in a past life, I had been hospitalised there. So after some rest I returned to Ronda.

The journey to Ronda is beautiful, rising gradually through the lovely mountains with some hair-raising drops to look down on. The town consists of the old walled town and the newer much larger town divided by a gorge clearly shown on Pat's sketch. The buildings are lovely and some of the house doors are exquisite, made with timber, metals and glass (see enclosed one of Pat's visions of a door on page 50, from around the time she received her sketch of the gorge, red roofs etc). People had started to settle there about 20,000 years ago, as can be seen by some of the cave paintings. It is a bewitching place with Arab cultural influence everywhere.

I walked around for 2½ hours just enjoying the beauty of the city when I discovered the Church of La Merced, a large church that had originally been built as a mosque. Inside it had an enormous statue of the Black Madonna, which is very common in this area. So I knelt and prayed by it. Almost immediately I became aware of Mary, my guide, speaking to me and she said: "You must go to the third bridge where there is a spring, you must stop being in a state of conflict, you must integrate all the things you know about yourself and especially the things you have learned at Aracena and Ronda". I asked why it was necessary to go to the spring and she replied: "You must integrate yourself. The energy at the spring will integrate you".

I had only realised that day that Ronda has 3 bridges connecting the 2 parts of the town and I had only been to the larger one – the one that was on Pat's sketch. Dazed at this further message I set off, climbing downwards on stone steps for some considerable way until I discovered the small third bridge. I walked on the bridge for a while, but could see no sign of water, except at the bottom of the gorge. I retraced my steps and there was the spring at the beginning of the bridge in an earth bank, a small but strong jet of crystal clear water coming out of a bank of rock and earth. It was obviously used for animals as it had a stone trough below it and someone had recently placed a fresh green leaf from where it was pouring, to create a spout to direct the water into the trough.

Again I was astonished, because on my previous visit I missed this part of Ronda completely and she was right again! I was beginning to become late for my coach for my return journey to my hotel. I had not got a container for water, so I splashed the water all over myself. It was a wonderful experience!

This was my last night in Spain because the next day I was flying back home. My Aracena and Ronda experiences became magical and insightful for Pat and myself and have convinced me about re-incarnation and parallel universes; and, that, there is so much more to learn and experience in our spiritual lives.

TRAPPED

I have waited and waited,
For what?
I don't know.
Soon after I was born,
I sensed something was going to happen,
But what?
I have never discovered.
In my teens,
I climbed mountains,
Amazing feelings of space and expectation,
Enjoying the fear,
A strange sense of liberation.
This wasn't it.

Newness in my life also gave me these feelings,
Fear and liberation:
New people,
New jobs,
New houses,
New places.
Always with fear,
And a desire for freedom,
A constant desire for change.
But each new experience,
Trapped me.

So I needed to escape,
To what?
To where?
To whom?

JOHN CONNOR

I find the place,
Job or person,
And then I am trapped,
Again.

Christianity was not the answer,
Neither was Buddhism,
Nor the Maharishi Teachings,
Atheism seemed empty and sterile.
Whatever I am seeking,
Has a Light,
A spiritual beacon,
To illuminate my soul.

Now in the twilight of my life,
My soul feels like a stone,
Trapped.
There is light and dark,
Too much dark,
Not enough light,
My soul struggles to be free,
Releasing its spiritual force slowly,
Liberating itself,
Through my poems.

My soul struggles to be free